TO:

_____

FROM:

_____

DATE:

_____

Compiled by Kathy Shutt.

ISBN 978-1-61626-192-4

Cover and interior design: ThinkPen Design

Published by Barbour Publishing, Inc., P.O. Box 719, Uhrichsville, Ohio 44683, www.barbourbooks.com

Our mission is to publish and distribute inspirational products offering exceptional value and biblical encouragement to the masses.

 Member of the Evangelical Christian Publishers Association

Printed in Malaysia.

Blessings for You,
GRADUATE

BARBOUR
PUBLISHING

The Lord will give you prosperity. . . .
The Lord will. . .bless all the work you do.

DEUTERONOMY 28:11–12 NLT

Today, as you celebrate your graduation,
please know that I am praying for you.
I'm thanking God for the gift He's given
the world through you—and I'm asking
Him to bless you today and always.

Use what talent you possess:
The world would be very silent if no birds
sang there except those that sang best.

HENRY VAN DYKE

Make the least ado
about your greatest gifts.
Be content to act,
and leave the talking to others.

BALTASAR GRACIAN

Act quickly; think slowly.

GREEK PROVERB

Every time you make a choice you are
turning the central part of you,
the part that chooses, into something
a little different than what it was before.

C. S. LEWIS

God asks no one whether he will accept life.
That is not the choice.
You must take it.
The only choice is how.

HENRY WARD BEECHER

Sometimes you may look
around and feel discouraged.
After all, you're just one person
in an enormous world.
But even if you change
only one tiny corner for
the better, you will have
changed the world forever.
Even the smallest actions can
affect the lives of many;
like pebbles tossed in a lake,
you never know where
the ripples will end.
So don't be afraid to try.
Dare to make a difference.

Ellyn Sanna

We can do anything we want if
we stick to it long enough.

HELEN KELLER

They can conquer who
believe they can.

RALPH WALDO EMERSON

We must believe we are gifted for
something, and that this thing,
at whatever cost, must be attained.

MADAME CURIE

"With God all things are possible."

So long as I am acting
from duty and conviction,
I am indifferent to taunts and
jeers. I think they will probably
do me more good than harm.

WINSTON CHURCHILL

Knowledge is proud that
it knows so much;
wisdom is humble that
it knows no more.

WILLIAM COWPER

Without the Way there is no going;
without the Truth there is no knowing;
without the Life there is no living.

THOMAS À KEMPIS

When you are right with God on the inside,
that "rightness" will express itself on the
outside. Living with integrity comes easily
when it flows from your heart.
Be true to God at the very core of your being.
That commitment is like a seed that will grow
and send out branches through your entire life.
And one day, those branches will bloom.

ELLYN SANNA

If a great thing can be done at all,
it can be done easily. But it is the kind
of ease with which a tree blossoms after
long years of gathering strength.

JOHN RUSKIN

The ultimate can only
be expressed in conduct.
Example moves the world
more than doctrine.

HENRY MILLER

What lies behind us and what
lies before us are tiny matters
compared to what lies within us.

RALPH WALDO EMERSON

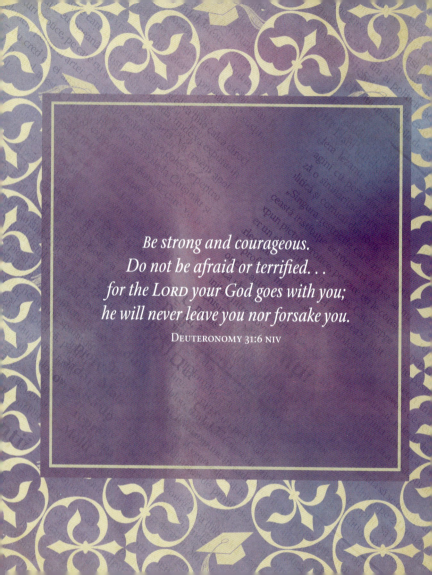

Be strong and courageous.
Do not be afraid or terrified...
for the LORD your God goes with you;
he will never leave you nor forsake you.

DEUTERONOMY 31:6 NIV

Choose your life with thought and
consideration. Don't let your life
be something that happens to you
while you're doing something else.
Decide what you want to put into life;
think about what you want to find in the
years ahead. . .and then make the choices
that will take you there. If you want a life that
includes a successful career, then work hard.
If you want a life that makes a difference,
that changes the world for the better,
then get involved. If you want a life that's
filled with love and friendships and family,
then be loving and caring and supportive in all
your relationships. Commit yourself to doing
the best job you can at whatever you do.

FAITH STEWART

We find in life exactly what we put into it.

RALPH WALDO EMERSON

Character building begins in
our infancy and continues
until our death.

ELEANOR ROOSEVELT

Some people try to avoid making choices
at all. They don't want to make the wrong
choice—and the consequences of even
the right choice can be frightening.
And so they try to walk the fence.
They think that way no one can
accuse them of anything.
But remember Pilate. He knew Jesus
was innocent. But Pilate didn't have
the courage to choose to do the right
thing. He washed his hands of making a
decision. And Jesus went to His death.
I pray that you will never be afraid
to take a stand. Stand up for right.
Make your choice known.

ELLYN SANNA

Only God can satisfy the hungry heart.

HUGH BLACK

I find the great thing in
this world is not so much
where we stand as in what
direction we are moving.

OLIVER WENDELL HOLMES

Wisdom is knowing what to do next.
Skill is knowing how to do it.
Virtue is doing it.

THOMAS JEFFERSON

"The joy of the Lord is your strength."

NEHEMIAH 8:10 NIV

As you head into the new life that lies ahead, you will doubtless change in countless ways. New responsibilities will bring you greater strength; new freedoms will allow you to develop fresh aspects of yourself. As your circumstances and environment change, you will adapt yourself in response. But you don't have to be passive as life shapes you. Instead, resolve to use each new phase in your life as an opportunity to grow. God has called you to do great things.

Ellyn Sanna

To change and to improve
are two different things.

German Proverb

Don't put off for tomorrow
what you can do today,
because if you enjoy it today,
you can do it again tomorrow.

James A. Michener

Success is to be measured not so much
by the position that one has reached
in life as by the obstacles which he
has overcome trying to succeed.

Booker T. Washington

Good character. . .is not given
to us. We have to build it piece
by piece—by thought, choice,
courage, and determination.

H. Jackson Brown

Integrity means your life is based on
truth. . .justice. . .and right living.
Integrity means you have a
conscience and listen to it.
Integrity defines the quality of your life.
Choose integrity and all its challenges.

Viola Ruelke Gommer

I get quiet joy from the observation
of anyone who does his job well.

WILLIAM FEATHER

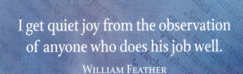

The roots of true achievement
lie in the will to become
the best you can be.

HAROLD TAYLOR

Joy comes from using your potential.

WILL SCHULTZ

Nothing great was ever
achieved without enthusiasm.

RALPH WALDO EMERSON

Do all the good you can
by all the means you can
in all the ways you can
in all the places you can
to all the people you can
as long as ever you can.

JOHN WESLEY

Let him that would move the
world first move himself.

SOCRATES

Aim high. Shoot for the stars.
Don't settle for anything less than your best.

ELLYN SANNA

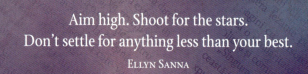

The beautiful is less what one
sees than what one dreams.

BELGIAN PROVERB

Let us believe that God is in all our simple
deeds and learn to find Him there.

A. W. TOZER

Live to shed joys on others.
Thus best shall your own
happiness be secured.

HENRY WARD BEECHER

Remember that when
you leave this earth,
you can take nothing that
you have received...but
only what you have been
given: a full heart enriched
by honest service, love,
sacrifice, and courage.

FRANCIS OF ASSISI

Keep away from people who try to belittle your ambitions. Small people always do that, but the really great make you feel that you, too, can become great.

MARK TWAIN

Sometimes life will seem to say: "You can never do it." "You're not good enough." "You'll never amount to much." Don't listen. God has a purpose for your life. Trust in Him—and believe in yourself.

ELLYN SANNA

In everything set them an example by doing what is good. In your teaching show integrity, seriousness and soundness of speech that cannot be condemned, so that those who oppose you may be ashamed because they have nothing bad to say.

Titus 2:7–8 NIV

If a man does not keep pace
with his companions,
perhaps it is because he hears
a different drummer. Let him
step to the music he hears,
however measured or far away.

HENRY DAVID THOREAU

As you walk along the path before you,
it may seem strange and new. You are not
alone. The One who made you watches over
you and guides your feet. He knows the way.

VIOLA RUELKE GOMMER

Live wholeheartedly; be surprised;
give thanks and praise. Then you will
discover the fullness of your life.

DAVID STEINDL-RAST

Keep a clear eye toward life's
end. Do not forget
your purpose and destiny
as God's creature.
What you are in His sight is
what you are and nothing more.

FRANCIS OF ASSISI

God wants to fit us perfectly in His plan,
if we allow Him to do so. He is willing to
bring all circumstances to bear to that
end. Ephesians 2:10 tells us that God has
already prepared, before the creation
of the world, the "good works" that He
wants us to do. . . . He doesn't have to look
around to see if He can find a job to fit my
qualifications when I decide to apply to
Him for employment! No. All is prepared.

HELEN ROSEVEARE

Life is like a baseball game.
You do not have to succeed
seven out of ten times, and you
can still make the all-star team.

ANONYMOUS

The remarkable truth is that our choices matter, not just to us and our own destiny but, amazingly, to God Himself and the universe He rules.

PHILIP YANCEY

"If you give, you will get! Your gift will return to you in full and overflowing measure, pressed down, shaken together to make room for more, and running over."

<small>LUKE 6:38 TLB</small>

I am only one, but I am still one;
I cannot do everything,
but I can still do something;
and because I cannot
do everything
I will not refuse to do the
something that I can do.

HELEN KELLER

Perhaps the most valuable result of an
education is the ability to make oneself do
the thing you have to do, whether you like it
or not. This is the first lesson to be learned.

THOMAS HENRY HUXLEY

The beginning is the most
important part of the work.

PLATO

It is the greatest of all
mistakes to do nothing
because you can only do a
little. Do what you can.

SYDNEY SMITH

Do what you can, with what you have, where you are.

THEODORE ROOSEVELT

Sometimes the size of the job will keep
you from acting. Like David looking up at
Goliath, you'll feel too little to fight
the giant that looms over you.
After all, the odds are clearly against you.
What's the point of even trying?
When those thoughts threaten to stop
you in your tracks, remember—David didn't
let Goliath's size stop him. Instead, he picked
up his little pebble and killed a giant.

ELLYN SANNA

Everything that is done in
this world is done by hope.

MARTIN LUTHER

Life is either a daring adventure or nothing.

HELEN KELLER

Imitate God, therefore, in everything you do. . . . Live a life filled with love, following the example of Christ.

EPHESIANS 5:1–2 NLT

You have a story, a story that you're living. So far, you've only lived the first few chapters. Much of what your story contains has been decided by the people in your life.

You didn't get to choose your family or where you would live or other aspects of your life.

But now you get to write the rest of your story; you get to choose what to do with what you've been given so far. It's kind of like one of those "choose your own adventure" books. And you will have adventures.

FAITH STEWART

And somehow you know that it won't be long before that beautiful creature will snap the lifeline that bound you together and soar as it was meant to soar. . .free and alone.

UNKNOWN

May you have the courage to let yourself drop into the hands of God.

ELLYN SANNA

Be like the bird that,
pausing in her flight awhile
on boughs too slight,
Feels them give way beneath
her wings and yet sings,
knowing that she hath wings.

VICTOR HUGO

To every man there openeth
a Way, and Ways, and a Way,
and the High Soul climbs the High Way,
and the Low Soul gropes the Low,
and in between, on the misty flats,
the rest drift to and fro.
But to every man there openeth
a High Way, and a Low.
And every man decideth
the Way his soul shall go.

JOHN OXENHAM

"Choose for yourselves this day whom you will serve. . . . But as for me. . .[I] will serve the Lord."

Joshua 24:15 NIV

Did you hear about the little mouse who
hitched a ride across a bridge on the back
of a huge elephant? When they got to the
other side, the mouse said, "Whew!
Did you see how we made that bridge shake?"
Deep down inside, you, too, want to
shake your world—but you have enough
sense to know you're no elephant.
Don't worry. God doesn't expect you to
be. In Ephesians 1:19 (NLT), Paul says,
"I also pray that you will understand
the incredible greatness of God's
power for us who believe him."
So hop on board. With God,
you can make a difference.
For eternity!

PATRICIA SOUDER

I dream for a living.

STEVEN SPIELBERG

The poor man is not he who
is without a cent but he
who is without a dream.

HARRY KEMP

Courage is the power of being mastered
and possessed with an idea.

Phillips Brooks

Keep thou thy dreams—
The tissue of all wings
Is woven first of them;
From dreams are made
The precious and
imperishable things,
Whose loveliness lives
on and does not fade.

VIRNA SHEARD

How much better to get wisdom than gold,
to choose understanding rather than silver!

Proverbs 16:16 niv

Choose a job you love, and you will
never have to work a day in your life.

Confucius

We grow by great dreams. All big men are dreamers. They see things in the soft haze of a spring's day or in the red fire of a long winter's evening. Some of us let these great dreams die, but others nourish and protect them, nurse them through bad days till they bring them to the sunshine and light which come always to those who sincerely hope that their dreams will come true.

WOODROW WILSON

Four things a man must learn to do
If he would keep his record true:
To think, without confusion, clearly;
To love his fellow man sincerely;
To act from honest motives purely;
To trust in God and Heaven securely.

HENRY VAN DYKE

Two roads diverged
in a wood and I—
I took the one less traveled by,
And that has made
all the difference.

ROBERT FROST

The way to God has been properly described as "letting oneself fall," and has been compared with the first flight of a baby eagle, pushed out of the nest by its parents, and then discovering to its amazement that the invisible ocean of light in which it is dropping is capable of bearing it up. The presence of God which surrounds everyone is like this invisible ocean which bears us up more surely than do all visible means of security.

KARL HEIM

I know not what the future holds, but I know who holds the future.

ANONYMOUS

Insist on yourself; never imitate.
Your own gift can present every moment
with the cumulative force of a whole life's
cultivation; but of the adopted talent of
another, you have only an extemporaneous
half-expression. That which each can do
best, none but his Maker can teach him.

RALPH WALDO EMERSON

Don't worry if you can't keep up
with the world's music.
Listen to God's song
in your own heart.
Stay in step with eternity.

ELLYN SANNA

*"Slowly, steadily, surely, the time approaches
when the vision will be fulfilled.
If it seems slow, wait patiently, for it will
surely take place. It will not be delayed."*

HABAKKUK 2:3 TLB

One man with belief is equal to
a thousand with only interests.

JOHN STUART MILL

Don't hide your gifts in the dark.
They'll do no one any good there,
least of all yourself.
Your own life will be
poorer than it needs to be.
It doesn't matter how your gifts
compare to those that others have
been given. God just wants you to use
whatever He's given you. And when you
do this, the world will be enriched.

ELLYN SANNA

Dear Lord, be good to me;
the sea is so wide and
my boat is so small.

IRISH FISHERMAN'S PRAYER

When one door of happiness closes,
another opens; but often we look so long
at the closed door that we do not see the
one which has been opened for us.

Helen Keller

Every person you meet knows something
you don't. Learn from them.

H. JACKSON BROWN

It is not enough to have
a good mind; the main
thing is to use it well.

RENE DESCARTES

In wisdom gathered over time I
have found that every experience
is a form of exploration.

ANSEL ADAMS

"Don't store up treasures here on earth. . . .
Wherever your treasure is,
there the desires of your heart will also be."

Matthew 6:19, 21 nlt

The important thing is not
to stop questioning.

ALBERT EINSTEIN

Oh, the thinks you can
think up if only you try!

DR. SEUSS

Everyone has talent. What is rare is the
courage to follow that talent. . .where it leads.

ERICA JONG

If Columbus had turned back, no one would have blamed him. Of course, no one would have remembered him either.

UNKNOWN

Doubt sees the obstacles;
faith sees the way.
Doubt sees the darkest night;
faith sees the day.
Doubt dreads to take a step;
faith soars on high.
Doubt questions, "Who believes?"
Faith answers, "I."

ANONYMOUS

Do not wait for great strength before setting out, for immobility will weaken you further. Do not wait to see very clearly before starting: One has to walk toward the light. Have you strength enough to take this first step? Courage enough to accomplish this small act. . .the necessity of which is apparent to you? Take this step! Perform this act! You will be astonished to feel that the effort accomplished, instead of having exhausted your strength, has doubled it. And that you already see more clearly what you have to do next.

PHILLIPE VERNIER

A ship in a harbor is safe, but that's not what ships are built for.

JOHN A. SHEDD

Did you ever see an unhappy
horse? Did you ever see a
bird that had the blues?
One reason why birds and
horses are not unhappy is
because they are not trying to
impress other birds and horses.

DALE CARNEGIE

Happiness is not in the destination;
it's in the journey.

DAN CLARK

On this special day of pride and
achievement, this is my prayer for you:

*"May the Lord bless you and protect you;
may the Lord's face be radiant with joy
because of you; may he be gracious to you,
show you his favor, and give you his peace."*

Numbers 6:24–26 TLB

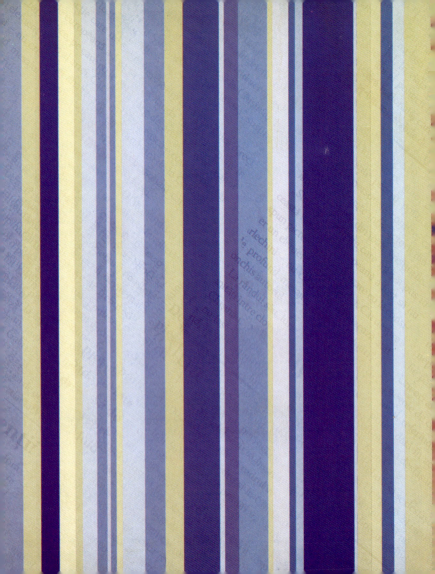